Communicating the Value of ESG: A Practical Guide for Communications Strategy Consultants

Copyright © 2024 Reginaldo Osnildo
All rights reserved.

PRESENTATION

INTRODUCTION TO ESG AND ITS IMPORTANCE

THE ROLE OF COMMUNICATION IN ESG

PREPARATION FOR ESG CONSULTANCY

PROSPECTING CONSCIOUS CUSTOMERS

INITIAL ANALYSIS OF THE CLIENT COMPANY

DEVELOPING AN ESG COMMUNICATION STRATEGY

EFFECTIVE NARRATIVES IN ESG COMMUNICATION

COMMUNICATION CHANNELS FOR ESG MESSAGES

STAKEHOLDER ENGAGEMENT

MEASURING THE IMPACT OF ESG COMMUNICATION

TRANSPARENT AND CREDIBLE ESG REPORTS

CRISIS MANAGEMENT AND ESG COMMUNICATION

INTERNAL COMMUNICATION ABOUT ESG PRACTICES

USE OF TECHNOLOGY IN ESG COMMUNICATION

STRATEGIC PARTNERSHIPS TO AMPLIFY ESG

ESG SPOKESPERSON TRAINING

CONTENT MARKETING AND ESG

ESG EVENTS AND INITIATIVES

VISUAL COMMUNICATION AND ESG

ADAPTING ESG COMMUNICATION TO THE GLOBAL CONTEXT

COMMON CHALLENGES IN ESG COMMUNICATION

FUTURE TRENDS IN ESG COMMUNICATION

BUILDING A CAREER IN ESG CONSULTING

THE JOURNEY TOWARDS EFFECTIVE ESG COMMUNICATION

REGINALDO OSNILDO

PRESENTATION

Welcome to " **Communicating the Value of ESG: A Practical Guide for Communications Strategy Consultants** ," your beacon in the increasingly essential world of Environmental, Social and Governance practices in companies. If you are a consultant or communications professional looking to not only understand, but also implement and improve effective communications strategies that raise the ESG profile of committed companies, this book is for you.

In this guide, I decided to bring together not only the knowledge accumulated through recognized studies and practices, but also my updated perception of what really works in today's dynamic corporate landscape. My goal is to make your journey not only informative, but also practical and directly applicable to your needs and those of the companies you work with. You will find here a clear and adaptable path to ensuring that ESG initiatives are not only understood, but also valued and supported by all stakeholders.

Through carefully structured chapters, this book will cover everything from introducing the concept of ESG and its undeniable importance in today's corporate world, to how to develop and implement communications strategies that truly resonate. Each chapter is designed to be complete in itself, offering you valuable insights and practical actions, always encouraging exploration of the next step on that journey.

As you progress through each chapter, you will be invited to reflect on how these strategies can be adapted and personalized to meet the specific needs of each company, always focusing on the positive impact that effective ESG communication can generate. From preparing as an ESG consultant, to prospecting for conscious clients, to developing effective narratives and engaging stakeholders, this book is your complete guide.

We are at a time when ESG practices are not just an option, but an urgent necessity for companies that want to prosper and be recognized as responsible leaders on the global stage. Therefore, I invite you to delve into this practical guide, enrich your knowledge and skills, and together, we can transform the landscape of corporate communication for a more sustainable and fair future.

By the end of this guide, I hope that you are not only equipped with the tools and knowledge to effectively communicate ESG values, but that you also feel inspired to be an agent of change in the success stories of companies and society as a whole. Now, allow me to guide you through the first step of this exciting journey with the next chapter: **"INTRODUCTION TO ESG AND ITS IMPORTANCE"**. This chapter will not only lay the foundation for everything that follows, but also illuminate the profound impact that well-communicated ESG practices can have in the corporate world and beyond.

So, are you ready to get started? Let's move forward, explore and shape the future of ESG communication together.

Yours sincerely

Reginaldo Osnildo

INTRODUCTION TO ESG AND ITS IMPORTANCE

In today's corporate world, the term ESG (Environmental, Social and Governance) has become more than a simple acronym; it represents a set of practices that reflect companies' commitment to sustainability and social responsibility. This chapter aims to offer you, dear reader, a comprehensive understanding of what ESG is, highlighting its growing relevance and the significant impact it has on brand perception in today's business environment.

WHAT IS ESG?

ESG is a criterion used to assess the degree to which an organization works conscientiously in relation to environmental, social and governance issues.

- **Environmental** concerns the practices that a company adopts to preserve the environment, including natural resource management, reduction of carbon emissions and sustainability.

- **Social** refers to the way the company treats people, ranging from the working conditions of its employees to the impact of its products and services on the community.

- **Governance** involves transparency in the company's operations, ethics in conducting business and the composition of its leadership.

THE IMPORTANCE OF ESG IN TODAY'S CORPORATE WORLD

The importance of ESG in the contemporary corporate landscape cannot be underestimated. Investors, consumers and employees are increasingly aware of ESG issues, demanding that companies not only pursue profits, but also contribute positively to the world. This translates into a number of tangible benefits for companies that adopt ESG practices, including:

- **Attracting investments:** Investors are increasingly allocating resources to companies with strong ESG practices, understanding that these criteria are indicative of long-term sustainability and lower risk.

- Customer loyalty: Consumers increasingly prefer products and services from companies that demonstrate concern for environmental and social issues, positively influencing brand perception.

- Talent attraction and retention: Employees, especially younger generations, seek to work in organizations that reflect their values, making ESG practices a crucial factor in attracting and retaining talent.

THE IMPACT ON BRAND PERCEPTION

Commitment to ESG has a profound impact on the way brands are perceived in the market. A well-implemented and effectively communicated ESG strategy can transform a company's image, positioning it as a conscious and responsible leader. This not only strengthens the loyalty of existing customers, but also attracts new customers who value sustainability and social responsibility.

By understanding what ESG is and its fundamental importance in the corporate world, you are now prepared to dive deeper into the intricate relationship between ESG and communication. In the next chapter, **"THE ROLE OF COMMUNICATION IN ESG,"** we will explore how effective communication strategies are vital for promoting and reporting on a company's ESG initiatives. You will learn how clear and impactful communication not only raises a company's ESG profile, but also engages stakeholders in a meaningful and constructive dialogue about sustainable practices.

As we move forward, remember: ESG knowledge is not just theoretical. It is a powerful tool for you to make a difference in the corporate world, creating not only economic, but also social and environmental value. Let's take the next step on this transformative journey together.

THE ROLE OF COMMUNICATION IN ESG

On the journey towards more conscious and responsible business action, communication takes on a leading role. This chapter is dedicated to exploring the vital importance of effective communication strategies for promoting and reporting on a company's ESG initiatives. We will uncover how communication not only amplifies the impact of these initiatives, but also strengthens the connection between companies and their stakeholders, opening paths for mutual understanding and meaningful engagement.

COMMUNICATION AS A BRIDGE

At the heart of ESG is the need to create a transparent and continuous dialogue between companies and different interest groups: from investors and consumers to the internal team itself and the surrounding community. Effective communication serves as a bridge, allowing ESG initiatives to not only be implemented, but also recognized, valued and supported by everyone.

TRANSMITTING ESG VALUES

Conveying a company's ESG values is a task that goes beyond simple reports or announcements. It requires a carefully planned and executed communication strategy capable of:

- **Clearly articulate ESG objectives:** It is essential that the company's ESG objectives are communicated in a clear and understandable way, avoiding jargon and making them relevant to different audiences.

- **Demonstrate commitment through stories:** People connect with stories. Presenting ESG initiatives through engaging narratives helps demonstrate the company's commitment in a tangible and memorable way.

- **Promote dialogue and feedback:** Communication about ESG must be bidirectional, encouraging feedback and dialogue with stakeholders. This not only increases transparency but also promotes a sense of participation and belonging.

OVERCOMING CHALLENGES IN ESG COMMUNICATION

One of the main challenges in ESG communication is avoiding the perception of "greenwashing" – the practice of making misleading claims about how green a company's practices are. To overcome this, it is essential that communication is based on concrete actions, evidence and measurable results. This requires:

- **Transparency:** Be open about successes and, equally important, areas that need improvement.

- **Consistency:** Maintain consistent communication about ESG initiatives, integrating them across all platforms and points of contact with stakeholders.

- **Credibility:** Support messages with verifiable data and, when possible, third-party certifications or evaluations.

Mastering the art of ESG communication is a crucial step for any professional involved in consultancy or communication strategy for companies committed to responsible practices. However, to apply these strategies effectively, it is essential to first understand and adequately prepare for the role of an ESG consultant.

In the next chapter, **"PREPARATION FOR ESG CONSULTANCY"**, we will delve into the world of preparation and training necessary to become a leading ESG consultant. You will discover valuable tips on training, necessary skills and market understanding that are key to guiding companies in implementing and communicating their ESG initiatives.

As we move forward, remember: effective ESG communication is not just about conveying information, but about building trust, inspiring action, and shaping perceptions. Together, let's discover how you can become a catalyst for positive change by using communication to amplify the impact of ESG practices.

PREPARATION FOR ESG CONSULTANCY

Becoming a qualified ESG consultant is a journey that demands not only a deep understanding of environmental, social and governance issues, but also a robust set of communication and strategy skills. This chapter is dedicated to guiding you through the essential steps to prepare for this challenging and rewarding career, focusing on training, necessary skills and understanding the market. Ultimately, you will be better equipped to help companies develop and communicate their ESG initiatives effectively.

BACKGROUND AND TRAINING

The foundation for a successful career in ESG consulting begins with a solid educational background. This does not necessarily mean that you need a specific degree in ESG (although specialized courses can be very valuable), but rather that you should pursue an education that covers the three pillars of ESG:

- **Environmental:** Knowledge of sustainability, environmental sciences and environmental policies.

- **Social:** Studies in human rights, social work, community development and business ethics.

- **Governance:** Training in corporate law, management ethics and business transparency.

In addition to academic training, participating in ESG workshops, seminars and online courses can complement your learning and keep you up to date with the latest practices and regulations.

REQUIRED SKILLS

To be an effective ESG consultant, you will need a diverse set of skills, including:

- **Critical analysis:** The ability to evaluate a company's ESG practices critically, identifying areas of strength and points in need of improvement.

- **Communication:** Exceptional communication skills are essential, both to convey ESG complexities in a clear and understandable way, and to build trusting relationships with stakeholders.

- **Strategy and planning:** Competence to develop ESG communication strategies that are aligned with the company's business objectives and that effectively involve stakeholders.

UNDERSTANDING THE MARKET

A deep understanding of the market and current trends in ESG is crucial. This includes being aware of local and global regulations, understanding consumer expectations and knowing industry best practices. Stay informed through sustainability reports, specialized publications and by participating in ESG networks and forums.

Now that you understand the basics of preparing to become an ESG consultant, the next chapter, "**PROSPECTING CONSCIOUS CUSTOMERS**," will guide you on how to identify and approach potential clients who value or need to improve their ESG practices. This step is vital to apply your skills and knowledge, positively impacting the corporate world through ESG.

As we move forward, remember: every company has its own needs and challenges regarding ESG. Your ability to adapt, understand and offer personalized solutions will be the key to success. Let's together explore how you can effectively connect with these clients and make a real difference through your work in ESG consulting.

PROSPECTING CONSCIOUS CUSTOMERS

Prospecting clients who value ESG practices is a crucial step for ESG-focused communications strategy consultants. This chapter aims to equip you with effective strategies for identifying and approaching these potential clients, who are essential to the success of your career as an ESG consultant. The key is to understand not only where to find these customers, but also how to communicate with them in ways that resonate with their values and needs.

IDENTIFYING POTENTIAL CUSTOMERS

Potential clients for ESG consulting can range from innovative startups looking to build a solid foundation in sustainable practices, to large corporations looking to improve their existing ESG initiatives. Identifying these customers involves:

- **Market research:** Use market research tools to identify industries and companies that are investing in sustainability and social responsibility.

- **Social networks and specialized forums:** Platforms like LinkedIn, as well as forums and groups dedicated to sustainable practices, are great places to find companies engaged with ESG issues.

- **ESG events and conferences:** Attending events focused on sustainability and social responsibility can offer valuable networking opportunities.

EFFECTIVE APPROACH

After identifying potential customers, the next step is to approach them effectively. Here are some tips to ensure your approach is successful:

- **Personalize your message:** Show that you've done your homework. Personalize your message by highlighting how your expertise and services can help the company achieve its specific ESG goals.

- **Emphasize tangible benefits:** Companies are interested in results. Highlight the tangible benefits of an effective ESG strategy, such as improving brand reputation, attracting investment and reducing operational costs.

- **Show success stories:** If possible, share case studies or examples of success where you helped other companies improve their ESG practices. This can increase your credibility and potential customer trust in your services.

ESTABLISHING RELATIONSHIPS OF TRUST

Building a trusting relationship begins with the first contact. Being transparent, demonstrating in-depth knowledge of ESG and showing commitment to client success are key to establishing a solid partnership. Remember, ESG consulting is a joint journey; Showing that you are invested for the long term can set you apart in the market.

With a clear understanding of how to prospect and approach conscientious customers, you are now more prepared to dive into the initial analysis of client companies. In the next chapter, "**INITIAL ANALYSIS OF THE CLIENT COMPANY**," we will explore how to conduct a detailed analysis of the company's current ESG practices and communication needs. This phase is critical for developing personalized, effective strategies that truly resonate with your client's values and goals.

As we move forward, remember that prospecting is just the beginning. The ability to deeply understand each client's specific needs and challenges is what will allow you to make a significant difference through your ESG consulting work. Let's continue on this journey together, preparing the ground for communication strategies that not only inform, but inspire and transform.

INITIAL ANALYSIS OF THE CLIENT COMPANY

After successful prospecting and establishing first contact with conscientious potential customers, the next essential step for the ESG consultant is to conduct a detailed initial analysis of the client company's ESG practices and its communication needs. This chapter will guide you on how to perform this analysis effectively, identifying areas of strength, opportunities for improvement, and communication strategies that align the company's ESG initiatives with its brand and business objectives.

UNDERSTANDING CORPORATE CULTURE AND EXISTING PRACTICES

The first step in the initial analysis is to dive deeply into the company's corporate culture and existing ESG practices. This involves:

- **Review of existing documentation:** Start by reviewing annual reports, sustainability reports, internal policies, and any other relevant documentation that can provide insights into the company's current ESG practices.

- **Key Stakeholder Interviews:** Conduct interviews with leadership team members, employees, and other stakeholders to understand their perceptions and experiences related to the company's ESG initiatives.

EVALUATING STRATEGIC ALIGNMENT

The analysis should also focus on how current ESG practices are aligned with the company's global business and communication strategy. Key questions include:

- **Are ESG objectives clearly defined and integrated into the company's business goals?**

- **Are there gaps between stated ESG practices and the company's actual actions?**

- **How are ESG initiatives currently communicated to internal and external stakeholders?**

IDENTIFYING OPPORTUNITIES AND CHALLENGES

Based on an understanding of corporate culture and strategic alignment, identify opportunities to reinforce the company's ESG practices and improve its communication. This may include:

- **Innovation opportunities:** Areas where the company can implement new ESG practices or projects to improve its environmental and social performance.

- **Communication challenges:** Points where current communication may be failing to effectively convey the company's ESG initiatives, whether due to lack of clarity, inconsistency or lack of engagement with stakeholders.

PREPARING AN ACTION PLAN

Based on your analysis, develop an initial action plan that addresses both improvements to ESG practices and communication strategies. This plan must:

- **Prioritize areas for action:** Identify which areas require immediate attention and which can be addressed in the medium and long term.

- **Define clear objectives:** Establish specific, measurable, achievable, relevant and time-bound (SMART) objectives for each area of action.

- **Recommend communication strategies:** Suggest effective methods for communicating ESG improvements and initiatives, both internally and externally.

With a deep understanding of your client company's ESG practices and an initial action plan in hand, you are now prepared to move towards developing a bespoke ESG communications strategy. In the next chapter, **"DEVELOPING AN ESG COMMUNICATION STRATEGY**," we will explore how to create a strategy that not only aligns the company's ESG practices with its business goals, but also effectively engages all stakeholders in the process.

This chapter will be essential in transforming your initial analysis into concrete actions that promote positive change. As we move forward, remember that analysis is just the beginning. The true art of ESG consulting lies in the ability to use these insights to inspire and implement strategies that make a real difference in the world.

DEVELOPING AN ESG COMMUNICATION STRATEGY

After an initial in-depth analysis of the client company's ESG practices and communications needs, the next crucial step is to develop an ESG communications strategy that not only aligns the company's practices with its business goals, but also effectively engages all stakeholders in this process. This chapter will provide a step-by-step guide to creating a comprehensive and effective ESG communications strategy.

DEFINING CLEAR ESG COMMUNICATION OBJECTIVES

The starting point for any effective communication strategy is to establish clear and measurable objectives. Ask yourself:

- **What does the company hope to achieve with its ESG communication?**

- **What specific messages does it need to communicate?**

- **How do these objectives align with your overall business goals and ESG practices?**

These goals can range from raising awareness about specific ESG initiatives to improving brand perception or engaging more deeply with stakeholders.

MAPPING STAKEHOLDERS

Understanding who your stakeholders are and what they value is crucial to developing an effective communications strategy. That includes:

- **Employees,** who can be motivated to contribute more actively to the company's ESG initiatives.

- **Customers,** whose purchasing preferences can be influenced by effective communication of ESG practices.

- **Investors,** who are increasingly looking to invest in companies with strong ESG credentials.

- **Local community** and **business partners,** who may be

affected or may benefit from the company's ESG practices.

DEVELOPING THE MESSAGE

The essence of any ESG communications strategy is the message it conveys. Messages must be:

- **Clear and consistent:** Avoid jargon and make sure messages are easily understood by all audiences.

- **Authentic:** Ensure that messages reflect the company's true ESG practices and avoid the risk of "greenwashing".

- **Adaptable:** Personalize messages for different audiences, keeping the essence of the message consistent.

Choosing the Appropriate Communication Channels

The selection of communication channels is essential to reach stakeholders effectively. This may include:

- **Annual and sustainability reports**

- **Social media**

- **Internal and external newsletters**

- **Events and workshops**

Each channel has its own strengths and should be chosen based on the target audience and communication objectives.

MEASURING AND ADJUSTING

Finally, it is vital to establish clear metrics to measure the success of your ESG communications strategy and be willing to adjust it as necessary. This may include social media engagement analytics, customer or employee satisfaction surveys, and media coverage.

With an ESG communications strategy developed and ready to implement, the next step is to ensure that the narratives created are authentic, engaging and, above all, effective in highlighting the company's ESG initiatives in a way that resonates with all stakeholders. In the next chapter, **"EFFECTIVE NARRATIVES IN ESG COMMUNICATION"**, we will delve into techniques for telling stories that not only inform, but also inspire and mobilize action, taking ESG communication to a new level.

Remember: an ESG communications strategy is not a static document, but a living plan that must evolve along with the company's ESG initiatives and stakeholder expectations. As we move forward, stay flexible, adaptable, and always on the lookout for opportunities to improve your strategy to ensure the greatest possible impact.

EFFECTIVE NARRATIVES IN ESG COMMUNICATION

The art of storytelling is a powerful tool in communicating ESG initiatives. Authentic, well-constructed stories have the potential to emotionally connect, educate and motivate action among stakeholders. This chapter is dedicated to exploring how to create and utilize effective narratives that highlight a company's ESG practices in ways that truly resonate with your audience.

THE IMPORTANCE OF AUTHENTICITY

At the heart of any effective ESG narrative is authenticity. Stories must reflect the company's true values and demonstrate a genuine commitment to sustainable and responsible practices. To achieve this, it is crucial:

- **Base narratives on real facts and actions:** Stories must be based on concrete ESG initiatives and measurable results, avoiding exaggerations or false promises.

- **Show vulnerability:** Admitting challenges and areas for improvement can increase credibility and trust with stakeholders.

BUILDING YOUR NARRATIVE

An effective ESG narrative generally follows a classic storytelling structure, consisting of:

- **Context:** Sets the scene and introduces the importance of ESG initiatives.

- **Challenge:** Presents a problem or challenge that the company faced in relation to ESG issues.

- **Action:** Describes the actions taken by the company to address the challenge.

- **Result:** Shows the results and positive impacts of the company's actions, both for the business and for society and the environment.

- **Vision for the future:** Points to future initiatives and how the company plans to continue its commitment to ESG practices.

INVOLVING STAKEHOLDERS

The most powerful ESG narratives are those that can meaningfully engage stakeholders. This can be achieved through:

- **Personalization:** Tailor your stories to resonate with different stakeholder groups, considering their interests and concerns.

- **Interactivity:** Encourage stakeholder involvement in narratives, whether through comments on social media platforms, participation in events or contributions to sustainability projects.

- **Visualization:** Use images, videos and infographics to make stories more engaging and easier to understand.

MEASURING THE IMPACT OF NARRATIVE

Assessing the effectiveness of your ESG narratives is critical to understanding their impact and identifying areas for improvement. This can be done through:

- **Stakeholder feedback:** Collect direct feedback through surveys or feedback sessions.

- **Engagement analysis:** Monitor engagement with your stories across social media platforms and other communication channels.

- **Impact on behavior:** Note any changes in stakeholder behavior or perceptions that can be attributed to the narratives.

With a deep understanding of how to build and utilize effective ESG narratives, the next chapter, "**COMMUNICATION CHANNELS FOR ESG MESSAGES**," will explore the selection and effective use of communication channels to disseminate your stories. Each channel offers unique opportunities to reach and engage your target audiences effectively.

Remember: powerful narratives are those that not only inform, but also inspire. As you move forward, consider how each story you tell can contribute to deeper understanding and greater support for your company's ESG initiatives, driving positive change inside and outside the organization.

COMMUNICATION CHANNELS FOR ESG MESSAGES

Selecting and effectively utilizing the right communication channels is essential to ensuring your ESG messages reach and engage stakeholders effectively. Each channel has its own particularities and may be more suitable for certain types of messages or target audiences. This chapter will cover how to choose the appropriate channels for your ESG communication strategies and how to maximize their impact.

EVALUATING COMMUNICATION CHANNELS

Channel selection should begin with a careful assessment of your target audiences and communication objectives. Some of the most common channels include:

- **Annual and sustainability reports:** Ideal for comprehensively communicating the company's ESG performance to investors and other interested parties.

- **Social media:** Excellent for reaching a broad and diverse audience, allowing interactivity and direct engagement.

- **Corporate website:** A central point to host detailed information about the company's ESG practices, accessible to all stakeholders.

- **Newsletters:** Useful for keeping internal and external stakeholders informed about regular updates on ESG initiatives.

- **Webinars and virtual events:** Provide a platform for in-depth discussions on ESG topics, promoting stakeholder education and engagement.

MAXIMIZING THE IMPACT OF COMMUNICATION CHANNELS

For each channel selected, consider the following strategies to maximize your impact:

- **Personalize the message:** Adapt your messages to suit the specificities and preferences of each channel's audience.

- **Create quality content:** Invest in attractive visual content and engaging stories that can capture attention and convey the message effectively.

- **Promote interaction:** Encourage feedback and dialogue with your audiences, especially on interactive platforms like social media.

- **Measure reach and engagement:** Use analytical tools to monitor the performance of your communications on each channel and adjust your strategies as necessary.

ETHICAL AND TRANSPARENCY CONSIDERATIONS

When communicating about ESG, it is essential to maintain a high standard of ethics and transparency. This means:

- **Avoid greenwashing:** Make sure your messages are honest and accurately reflect the company's ESG practices.

- **Be clear and direct:** Avoid jargon and communicate clearly to ensure your messages are understood by all audiences.

- **Publicize progress and challenges:** Share both the successes and challenges faced in ESG initiatives, promoting an image of authenticity and trust.

With a solid strategy for selecting and utilizing ESG communication channels, you are ready to move to the next stage: stakeholder engagement. In the next chapter, **"STAKEHOLDER ENGAGEMENT"**, we will explore effective methods for engaging different stakeholder groups, including employees, customers, investors and local communities, in ESG initiatives.

Remember: choosing and effectively using communication channels is critical to ensuring your ESG messages not only reach, but also resonate with your audiences. As we proceed, think about how each channel can be optimized to create deeper, more meaningful connections with stakeholders, fostering broader understanding and support for the company's ESG initiatives.

STAKEHOLDER ENGAGEMENT

Effective stakeholder engagement is critical to the success of ESG initiatives. This chapter explores methods for engaging diverse stakeholder groups—employees, customers, investors, and local communities—ensuring that they not only understand, but also support and actively participate in a company's ESG practices. Each group has its own expectations and needs, requiring a personalized approach to maximize engagement.

EMPLOYEES: CULTIVATING BRAND AMBASSADORS

- **Internal communication:** Use internal communication channels, such as newsletters and team meetings, to share updates on ESG initiatives and celebrate achievements.

- **Involvement in ESG projects:** Encourage employee participation in ESG projects, allowing them to contribute ideas and lead initiatives.

- **Training and education:** Offer regular training on the importance of ESG and how each employee can play an active role.

CUSTOMERS: BUILDING RELATIONSHIPS BASED ON VALUES

- **Clear communication:** Ensure that information about the company's ESG practices is easily accessible and understandable to customers, highlighting how these practices add value to products or services.

- **Feedback and dialogue:** Establish channels for customers to share feedback on ESG initiatives, using this information to continually improve.

- **Awareness campaigns:** Develop campaigns that educate customers about ESG issues and how their support makes a difference.

INVESTORS: ALIGNING INTERESTS FOR SUSTAINABLE INVESTMENTS

- **Transparent reporting:** Provide detailed and transparent reporting on ESG performance, demonstrating how it aligns with the company's long-term objectives and return potential.

- **Direct communication:** Maintain an open line of communication with investors to discuss ESG strategies and listen to their expectations and concerns.

- **Demonstration of value:** Show how ESG initiatives contribute to the company's resilience and financial sustainability.

LOCAL COMMUNITIES: FOSTERING POSITIVE PARTNERSHIPS

- **Community impact projects:** Engage in projects that directly benefit local communities, whether through environmental initiatives or social development programs.

- **Open dialogue:** Establish forums to listen to the concerns of local communities and seek joint solutions to ESG issues.

- **Transparency in operations:** Be transparent about the impact of the company's operations on the local community and how it is working to minimize it or transform it into a positive impact.

With a strategic approach to stakeholder engagement, the next step is to measure the impact of these ESG communication strategies. In the next chapter, "**MEASURING THE IMPACT OF ESG COMMUNICATION**", we will explore tools and metrics to evaluate the effectiveness of communication strategies, allowing for continuous adjustments and improvements.

Remember: engaging stakeholders is not just about informing them about ESG initiatives, but also about inspiring them to actively participate in these initiatives. As you move forward, consider how each interaction can strengthen your commitment to ESG practices and create an expanded support network for your company's sustainability goals.

MEASURING THE IMPACT OF ESG COMMUNICATION

To ensure that ESG communication strategies are not only effective, but also continually evolving and improving, it is essential to measure their impact. This chapter explores the tools and metrics that can be used to evaluate the effectiveness of ESG communication strategies, enabling companies to adjust their approaches according to the results obtained.

DEFINING SUCCESS METRICS

The first step to measuring the impact of ESG communication is to define clear and objective metrics of success. These may include:

- **Reach and engagement:** Analyzing reach and engagement across social media, websites and newsletters provides insights into how much your ESG messages are being seen and how effective they are in generating interactions.

- **Changes in brand perception:** Brand perception surveys can help measure changes in how stakeholders view the company in relation to its ESG initiatives.

- **Direct feedback:** Feedback collected through surveys, discussion forums and other direct channels can provide a qualitative assessment of the impact of ESG communication.

USING ANALYSIS TOOLS

Several analytical tools can be employed to collect and analyze data on the impact of ESG communication:

- **Social media analysis tools:** Allows you to monitor engagement, such as likes, shares, comments and views, offering insight into how much ESG messages are resonating with the public.

- **Website analytics software:** Provides data about website visitors, including time spent on specific ESG-related pages, bounce rates and conversions, helping you understand visitors' interest in ESG initiatives.

- **Online surveys and questionnaires:** Survey tools can be used to collect direct feedback from stakeholders about ESG initiatives and communication effectiveness.

INTERPRETING DATA AND ADJUSTING STRATEGIES

After collecting data, the next step is to interpret it in order to understand the real impact of ESG communication strategies and identify areas for improvement. Important questions to consider include:

- **Which communication channels are being most effective?**

- **Are there specific messages that are generating more engagement or positive reactions?**

- **How can collected data inform adjustments to communications strategies to improve engagement and reach?**

With strategies for measuring the impact of ESG communications well established, the next step is to ensure that sustainability reporting and ESG communications are transparent and credible in the eyes of stakeholders. In the next chapter, **"TRANSPARENT AND CREDIBLE ESG REPORTS**," we will explore how to prepare and present reports that not only comply with regulatory and market standards, but also build trust and reinforce a company's commitment to sustainability.

Remember: measuring impact is a crucial part of the ESG communication cycle, providing valuable insights that allow you to continually optimize your strategies to achieve the best possible results. As we move forward, stay focused on how each insight can be used to improve communication, engagement and, ultimately, the impact of your company's ESG initiatives.

TRANSPARENT AND CREDIBLE ESG REPORTS

In the journey to effectively communicate ESG initiatives, the transparency and credibility of ESG reporting play vital roles. These reports not only serve as a window into the company's sustainability practices, but also as a demonstration of the organization's commitment to transparency and corporate responsibility. This chapter will cover how to prepare and present ESG reports that comply with regulatory and market standards, building trust and reinforcing commitment to sustainability.

ESTABLISHING THE BASIS FOR TRANSPARENT REPORTING

Transparency begins with adopting recognized standards and frameworks for ESG reporting, such as GRI (Global Reporting Initiative), SASB (Sustainability Accounting Standards Board) and TCFD (Task Force on Climate-related Financial Disclosures). Using these standards as a basis ensures that reports are comparable, reliable and relevant to stakeholders.

ELEMENTS OF A CREDIBLE ESG REPORT

An effective ESG report must include:

- **Declaration of commitment:** A message from the company's leadership reaffirming the commitment to sustainability.

- **Governance:** Description of how sustainability is governed within the organization, including accountability structures and decision-making processes.

- **Strategy and objectives:** Clear alignment between the company's ESG strategy and its long-term business objectives.

- **Performance and impact:** Quantitative and qualitative details about the company's performance against its ESG objectives, including environmental, social and governance impacts.

- **Risks and opportunities:** Analysis of ESG-related risks and opportunities faced by the company and how they are being addressed.

- **Case studies and stories:** Concrete examples of ESG initiatives in action, highlighting successes, challenges and learnings.

- **Future plans:** Vision on how the company plans to continue advancing its ESG practices.

GUARANTEING CREDIBILITY

For an ESG report to be considered credible, it must:

- **Be evidence-based:** All claims and data presented must be easily verifiable and based on concrete evidence.

- **Include external verification:** Where possible, include third-party audits or verifications to validate the information in the report.

- **Be transparent about challenges:** Don't hide difficulties or failures. Being open about challenges increases stakeholders' trust in the company's sincerity.

Understanding the importance and methodology behind creating transparent and credible ESG reports, the next stage is to face adverse situations with the same integrity. In the next chapter, **"CRISIS MANAGEMENT AND ESG COMMUNICATION"**, we will cover strategies for managing crises related to ESG issues and how to effectively communicate the company's response to such events.

Remember: ESG reports are a bridge of trust between the company and its stakeholders. They not only reflect past and present performance, but also signal future commitment to sustainable and responsible business practices. As you move forward, stay focused on reinforcing transparency and credibility in all forms of ESG communication.

CRISIS MANAGEMENT AND ESG COMMUNICATION

Crisis management related to Environmental, Social and Governance (ESG) issues is a critical component in a company's resilience and long-term sustainability. This chapter will cover effective strategies for managing ESG crises and how to proactively communicate the company's response, maintaining stakeholder trust and support even in challenging times.

PREPARATION BEFORE THE CRISIS

The best crisis management starts long before a crisis arises. That includes:

- **ESG risk assessment:** Proactively identify ESG risks that the company may face and assess their potential impact.

- **Crisis response plans:** Develop specific response plans for different ESG crisis scenarios, including clear chains of command and communication procedures.

- **Training and simulations:** Conduct regular training and crisis simulations with key teams to ensure they are prepared to act efficiently.

RESPONDING TO A CRISIS

When a crisis occurs, speed and clarity in communication are essential. The following steps can help guide your response:

- **Fast internal communication:** Inform internal teams about the crisis and the action plan, ensuring that everyone speaks the same language.

- **Initial public statement:** Issue a public statement as soon as possible, acknowledging the crisis and expressing commitment to dealing with the situation in a transparent and responsible manner.

- **Regular Updates:** Provide regular updates on crisis resolution efforts, both internally and externally.

- **Support for those affected:** Show support and offer

solutions to those directly affected by the crisis.

COMMUNICATING THE RESPONSE

The way a company communicates during and after a crisis can have a significant impact on stakeholder perception. Consider:

- **Transparency:** Be transparent about what went wrong, the actions taken to correct the problem and what will be done to prevent future crises.

- **Responsibility:** Take responsibility for the crisis, avoiding blaming third parties or external circumstances.

- **Commitment to improvements:** Clearly communicate plans to improve practices and prevent the recurrence of the crisis.

LEARNING FROM THE CRISIS

After the crisis is resolved, it is crucial to analyze what happened, what went well or poorly in the response, and how crisis management and communication plans can be improved. This may include:

- **Review and analysis:** Conduct a complete review of crisis management and communications effectiveness.

- **Updates to crisis plans:** Update crisis management and communication plans based on lessons learned.

- **Communication of learning:** Share learning with stakeholders, reinforcing the commitment to continuous improvement.

Having established solid strategies for crisis management and ESG communication, the next step is to incorporate these practices of responsibility and transparency into the company's internal culture. In the next chapter, "**INTERNAL COMMUNICATION ABOUT ESG PRACTICES**", we will explore the importance of communicating and cultivating the ESG culture within the company, involving all organizational levels.

Remember: Effective ESG crisis management not only protects the company from immediate harm, but also reinforces its commitment to long-term sustainability and responsibility. As you move forward, focus on building resilience, trust, and transparency across all of your ESG practices.

INTERNAL COMMUNICATION ABOUT ESG PRACTICES

Effective internal communication of ESG practices is fundamental to cultivating a corporate culture that values sustainability and social responsibility. This chapter explores the importance of involving all organizational levels in ESG initiatives, ensuring that staff are not only informed about the company's actions, but also motivated to contribute to these efforts.

ESTABLISHING INTERNAL ESG COMMUNICATION CHANNELS

The first step to effective internal communication is to establish channels dedicated to ESG practices, such as:

- **Corporate intranet:** Dedicated ESG sections on the intranet can provide regular updates, educational resources and highlight internal success stories.

- **Meetings and workshops:** Regular meetings or workshops on ESG topics encourage open dialogue and sharing of ideas between teams.

- **Internal newsletters:** ESG-focused newsletters can highlight initiatives, progress and ways for employees to actively participate.

PROMOTING ESG CULTURE

For internal communication to be effective, it is essential that sustainability and social responsibility are integrated into the corporate culture:

- **Leadership by example:** Leadership must demonstrate a genuine commitment to ESG practices, communicating their importance and setting an example.

- **Recognition and rewards:** Implement recognition programs that reward employees' contributions to the company's ESG goals.

- **Training and development:** Offer training opportunities that allow employees to acquire new skills related to sustainability and social responsibility.

ENGAGE AND EMPOWER EMPLOYEES

An effective internal ESG communications strategy not only informs, but also engages and empowers employees to take action:

- **ESG working groups:** Create ESG working groups or committees that allow employees to actively participate in the development and implementation of initiatives.

- **Feedback channels:** Establish channels where employees can express their ideas and concerns about ESG practices, promoting an inclusive and collaborative work environment.

- **Voluntary initiatives:** Encourage and facilitate employee involvement in voluntary initiatives that support the company's ESG objectives.

MEASURING IMPACT

To assess the effectiveness of internal communication about ESG practices, it is important to measure the impact of these strategies:

- **Employee engagement surveys:** Conduct regular surveys to measure the level of employee understanding and engagement with ESG practices.

- **Participation analysis:** Monitor participation in workshops, training programs and voluntary initiatives to assess the level of active involvement of employees.

By establishing strong internal communication about ESG practices, the company is well positioned to explore the next stage: utilizing technology in ESG communication. In the next chapter, "**USE OF TECHNOLOGY IN ESG COMMUNICATION**", we will explore how digital tools and platforms can be used to further enhance ESG communication, both internally and externally.

Remember: a well-informed and engaged team is the foundation for the success of ESG initiatives. As you move forward, focus on strengthening this foundation by creating an environment where every employee feels an integral part of the company's ESG journey.

USE OF TECHNOLOGY IN ESG COMMUNICATION

Integrating technology into ESG communication can transform the way companies share their sustainability and social responsibility initiatives, both internally and externally. This chapter discusses how digital tools and platforms can be used to amplify ESG messages, facilitate stakeholder engagement, and optimize ESG information management processes.

DIGITAL PLATFORMS FOR ENGAGEMENT AND EDUCATION

Using digital platforms offers an interactive way to engage stakeholders with the company's ESG initiatives:

ESG websites and microsites : Create a dedicated section or microsite for ESG on the corporate website, where interested parties can find detailed information, sustainability reports, and regular updates.

- **Mobile applications:** Develop applications that allow users to access ESG information, participate in sustainability initiatives and receive notifications about new projects or events.

SOCIAL NETWORKS TO EXPAND MESSAGE

Social media is a powerful tool for amplifying ESG messages, enabling companies to reach a broad and diverse audience:

- **Thematic campaigns:** Launch social media campaigns focused on specific ESG themes, using hashtags to increase visibility and encourage engagement.

- **Stories and videos:** Share success stories and videos that highlight the company's ESG initiatives, making content more accessible and engaging.

INTERNAL COLLABORATION TOOLS

Internal communication about ESG can be improved by using online collaboration tools:

- **Collaboration platforms:** Use platforms such as Slack,

Microsoft Teams or Google Workspace to create channels dedicated to ESG, facilitating the exchange of information and collaboration on projects.

- **Webinars and virtual meetings:** Organize webinars and virtual meetings to discuss ESG initiatives, provide training and promote a culture of sustainability within the organization.

DATA ANALYSIS FOR INFORMED STRATEGIES

Technology can be used to collect and analyze data related to ESG practices, helping companies make informed decisions:

- **Analytical tools:** Implement analytical tools to measure the impact and reach of ESG communications, identify trends, and adjust strategies as needed.

- **ESG management software:** Adopt ESG management software to track progress towards sustainability goals and generate detailed reports.

With the strategies and technology tools in place for effective ESG communication, the next step is to explore how to form strategic partnerships to further amplify the impact of ESG initiatives. In the next chapter, "**STRATEGIC PARTNERSHIPS TO AMPLIFY ESG**", we will discuss how collaborations with NGOs, educational institutions and other organizations can reinforce and validate a company's ESG practices.

Remember: technology is a powerful ally in ESG communication, offering new ways to interact, inform and engage. As you proceed, consider how each tool and platform can be used to not only disseminate your messages, but also to foster meaningful dialogue and promote action for sustainability and social responsibility.

STRATEGIC PARTNERSHIPS TO AMPLIFY ESG

Forming strategic partnerships is an effective way to amplify ESG initiatives, enabling companies to significantly expand their reach and impact. This chapter discusses how collaborations with NGOs, educational institutions, other companies and organizations can reinforce and validate ESG practices, as well as bring new perspectives and resources to the company.

IDENTIFYING POTENTIAL PARTNERS

The search for strategic partners should begin with a careful assessment of the company's ESG objectives and how a partnership can help achieve them. Potential partners could include:

- **Environmental and social NGOs:** Non-governmental organizations focused on environmental or social issues can offer expertise, credibility and access to support networks.

- **Educational institutions:** Universities and technical schools can be valuable sources of research, innovation and motivated young talent.

- **Companies with similar values:** Partnerships with other companies that share ESG commitments can lead to collaborative projects and the sharing of best practices.

DEVELOPING MUTUALLY BENEFICIAL RELATIONSHIPS

For a partnership to be successful, it is essential that both partners see clear benefits from the collaboration. This may include:

- **Joint projects:** Develop projects that align the company's ESG objectives with the missions of its partners, such as reforestation initiatives or community education programs.

- **Resource sharing:** Exchange knowledge, technologies or resources that can benefit both partners.

- **Joint awareness campaigns:** Launch marketing or awareness campaigns that highlight joint work and promote

ESG goals.

COMMUNICATING THE PARTNERSHIP

Communication about the partnership is crucial to ensure that stakeholders recognize and value joint efforts. Strategies include:

- **Joint announcements:** Use communication channels from both parties to announce the partnership and its objectives.

- **Progress reports:** Share regular updates on the progress of joint projects, highlighting successes and learnings.

- **Case studies:** Develop detailed case studies on specific projects to illustrate the impact of the partnership.

ASSESSING THE IMPACT OF THE PARTNERSHIP

To ensure that the partnership is achieving its ESG objectives, it is important to establish clear evaluation metrics and conduct periodic reviews of the collaboration's impact. This may include:

- **Environmental and social impact measures:** Assess the direct impact of joint projects on specific environmental or social issues.

- **Stakeholder feedback:** Collect feedback from internal and external stakeholders on the perception and effectiveness of the partnership.

- **ESG ROI Analysis:** Evaluate the return on investment in terms of improvements in ESG metrics and brand perception.

With strategies to form and leverage well-established strategic partnerships, the next step is to focus on internal development, preparing company leaders and spokespersons to effectively communicate ESG practices. In the next chapter, " **ESG SPOKESPERSON TRAINING** ", we will explore how to prepare individuals within the organization to represent the company and its ESG initiatives in a confident and informed way.

Remember: Strategic partnerships are a powerful amplifier for ESG initiatives, not only increasing the impact of a company's actions but also building a support network that transcends organizational boundaries. As we move forward, consider how these collaborations can enrich and expand your company's commitment to sustainability and social responsibility.

ESG SPOKESPERSON TRAINING

Success in communicating ESG initiatives depends significantly on the skill and preparation of the company's spokespersons. These individuals, whether they are executive leaders, sustainability managers or other designated employees, play a crucial role in representing the company and its ESG practices to the public, media and other stakeholders. This chapter focuses on how to effectively prepare ESG spokespersons, ensuring they communicate in a way that is confident, informed, and aligned with the company's values and strategies.

IDENTIFYING ESG SPOKESPERSONS

The selection of ESG spokespersons must be careful, looking for individuals who:

- **Demonstrate commitment to ESG:** Choose those who genuinely support ESG practices and can talk about them passionately.

- **Have communication skills:** Make sure they have good public communication skills and are able to convey complex messages clearly and concisely.

- **Represent diversity:** Spokespeople must reflect the diversity of the company and its community, ensuring that diverse perspectives are considered and respected.

DEVELOPING A TRAINING PROGRAM

An effective training program for ESG spokespersons should address:

- **Basic knowledge of ESG:** Ensure that all spokespersons have a solid understanding of ESG concepts and how they are applied within the company.

- **Crisis communication:** Prepare spokespeople to deal with difficult questions and crisis situations, teaching communication techniques under pressure.

- **Presentation and interview skills:** Provide training in presentation skills and conducting interviews, including how to respond to unexpected or challenging questions.

KEY MESSAGES AND CONSISTENCY

It is vital to ensure all spokespersons are aligned with the company's key ESG messages, including:

- **Development of key messages:** Create a set of key messages that all spokespersons should know and use to ensure consistency across all communications.

- **Regular updates:** Provide spokespeople with regular updates on ESG initiatives, progress and strategy changes so they are always informed.

PRACTICE AND FEEDBACK

Practice is an essential part of training, including:

- **Simulated interviews and presentations:** Conduct practice sessions that simulate real interviews and presentations about ESG.

- **Constructive feedback:** Provide constructive feedback after practice sessions, focusing on areas of improvement and reinforcing strengths.

With well-trained spokespeople prepared to communicate the company's ESG initiatives, the next step is to integrate these practices into the company's overall marketing and communications. In the next chapter, "**CONTENT MARKETING AND ESG**," we'll discuss how to use content marketing to educate, inform, and engage audiences about your company's ESG initiatives.

Remember: ESG spokespeople are the human face of your company's sustainability initiatives. They have the power to not only communicate, but also to inspire action and drive positive change. As you move forward, focus on keeping these individuals well-informed, supported, and ready to highlight your company's commitment to a more sustainable future.

CONTENT MARKETING AND ESG

Content marketing emerges as a powerful tool for companies looking to not only inform, but also engage their audiences around ESG initiatives. By creating content that is both informative and inspiring, companies can raise awareness about their sustainable practices, promote a responsible brand image and encourage action among consumers, investors and other stakeholders. This chapter explores how to effectively integrate ESG into your company's content marketing.

DEFINING ESG CONTENT STRATEGY

An ESG-focused content marketing strategy must start with a clear understanding of the company's goals in sustainability and social responsibility, as well as the expectations and interests of its audience. Essential elements include:

- **Identify core themes:** Base content strategy on ESG topics that are central to the company's mission and values, and that resonate with your audience.

- **Set clear objectives:** Establish what the company hopes to achieve with its ESG content marketing, whether that's raising awareness about specific initiatives, educating the public about sustainability issues, or promoting sustainable actions.

CREATING ENGAGING AND AUTHENTIC CONTENT

ESG content must be both engaging and authentic to capture attention and gain audience trust:

- **Stories of impact:** Share real stories about the impact of the company's ESG initiatives, highlighting success stories and learnings.

- **Educational content:** Produce blog articles, videos and infographics that educate the public about environmental, social and governance issues, and how individual and corporate actions can make a difference.

- **Transparency:** Be transparent about challenges and progress in ESG goals, building an honest narrative about the company's sustainability journey.

DIVERSIFYING CONTENT FORMATS

To reach a broad audience and engage them in different ways, diversify your content formats:

- **Videos and webinars:** Leverage the power of videos and webinars to tell engaging visual stories or educate on ESG topics.

- **Case studies and reports:** Develop detailed case studies and reports that delve into specific ESG initiatives and their impacts.

- **Posts on social networks:** Use social networks to share ESG content quickly and widely, encouraging sharing and discussion.

MEASURING SUCCESS

To evaluate the effectiveness of your ESG content marketing strategy, it is important to establish success metrics and monitor performance regularly. This may include:

- **Engagement analysis:** Monitor engagement with ESG content on social networks, blogs and other digital channels.

- **Audience feedback:** Collect and analyze direct audience feedback on ESG content, using this information to adjust strategy as needed.

- **Impact on brand perception:** Evaluate how ESG content marketing affects the brand's overall perception and sustainability reputation.

By implementing a solid and effective ESG content marketing strategy, the company sets the stage to further highlight its sustainability initiatives and engagement. In the next chapter, **"ESG EVENTS AND INITIATIVES,"** we will explore how to organize and execute events that advance the company's ESG initiatives and actively engage stakeholders.

Remember: ESG content marketing is not just a way to communicate what the company is doing in terms of sustainability; It is an opportunity to inspire action, promote positive change and strengthen connections with stakeholders through shared values.

ESG EVENTS AND INITIATIVES

Specific events and initiatives are excellent ways to highlight a company's commitment to ESG practices, create awareness, and engage stakeholders in a direct and meaningful way. This chapter covers how to plan and execute events that not only promote a company's ESG initiatives, but also encourage active participation from employees, customers, investors, and the local community.

ESG EVENT PLANNING

Careful planning is essential to ensure ESG events are successful and generate the desired impact. Important considerations include:

- **Goal setting:** Clarify what you hope to achieve with the event, whether that's raising awareness about a specific initiative, encouraging sustainable actions, or engaging the community.

- **Target audience:** Identify who you want to reach with the event and adapt the content and format to meet their expectations and interests.

- **Event format:** Decide whether the event will be in-person, virtual or hybrid, considering the desired reach and logistical restrictions.

TYPES OF ESG EVENTS AND INITIATIVES

There are several types of events and initiatives that can be organized to promote ESG practices:

- **Educational workshops and seminars:** Focused on educating participants about sustainability issues and how they can contribute to positive action.

- **Corporate volunteer days:** Encourage employees and community members to get directly involved in local sustainability or social responsibility projects.

- **Sustainability fairs:** Exhibit sustainable products or

innovations and promote discussions about green and responsible business practices.

- **Awareness campaigns:** Specific initiatives to raise awareness about critical environmental or social issues, often aligned with commemorative dates or international awareness days.

STAKEHOLDER ENGAGEMENT

To maximize the impact of ESG events and initiatives, it is crucial to effectively engage stakeholders:

- **Pre-event communication:** Use all available channels to promote the event in advance, highlighting the importance of the topic and how participants can benefit.

- **Active participation:** Encourage active participation during the event, whether through Q&A sessions, interactive workshops or group activities.

- **Post-event feedback:** Collect feedback from attendees to evaluate the success of the event and identify areas for improvement.

MEASURING IMPACT

Assessing the impact of ESG events is critical to understanding their success and how they can be improved in the future:

- **Participation analysis:** Monitor the number of participants and the level of engagement during the event.

- **Qualitative feedback:** Analyze participants' perceptions and suggestions to understand the value added by the event.

- **Long-term impact:** Evaluate the sustained impact of the event on the company's ESG practices and stakeholder perception.

After successfully running ESG events and initiatives, the next step is to incorporate these efforts into the company's visual communications and multimedia strategies. In the next chapter, " **VISUAL COMMUNICATION AND ESG**", we will explore the importance of visual design and multimedia in communicating ESG messages effectively and attractively.

Remember: ESG events and initiatives are opportunities not only to educate and engage, but also to demonstrate your company's commitment to sustainability and social responsibility in concrete actions. As you move forward, focus on creating events that inspire, inform, and catalyze positive change within and outside the organization.

VISUAL COMMUNICATION AND ESG

Visual communication plays a key role in making ESG messages more accessible, engaging and memorable to a broad audience. Effectively utilizing graphic design, videos and other visual elements can significantly amplify the impact of ESG initiatives, facilitating stakeholder understanding and engagement. This chapter explores strategies for integrating visual communications into ESG practices, highlighting the importance of visual aesthetics and multimedia.

THE IMPORTANCE OF VISUAL COMMUNICATION IN ESG

- **Increased understanding:** Visual elements can help simplify complex ESG concepts, making them easier for audiences to understand.

- **Increased engagement:** Compelling visual content is more likely to be noticed and shared, increasing the reach and engagement of ESG messages.

- **Message reinforcement:** Images and videos can reinforce written messages, helping stakeholders retain important information about ESG initiatives.

DEVELOPING EFFECTIVE VISUAL CONTENT

When developing visual content for ESG communication, consider the following elements:

- **Authenticity:** Ensure that visual content genuinely reflects the company's ESG initiatives and values, avoiding generic images that may appear disconnected or insincere.

- **Clarity and simplicity:** Drawings and graphics must be clear and easy to interpret, conveying the message without overloading the viewer with complex information.

- **Visual story:** Use visual narratives to tell the story of the company's ESG initiatives, creating an emotional connection with the audience.

USING MULTIPLE CHANNELS FOR VISUAL DISSEMINATION

To maximize the impact of ESG visual content, it is important to distribute it across multiple channels:

- **Social media:** Platforms such as Instagram, Facebook and Twitter are ideal for sharing images and videos that highlight ESG practices.

- **Corporate websites and blogs:** Incorporating visual elements into blog posts and web pages dedicated to ESG can enrich the user experience and provide deeper insights.

- **Reports and presentations:** Include charts, infographics and photos in ESG reports and presentations to make them more visually appealing and informative.

MEASURING THE IMPACT OF VISUAL CONTENT

To evaluate the effectiveness of visual content in communicating ESG messages, consider:

- **Engagement analysis:** Monitor engagement with visual content on social media and other channels, including likes, shares and comments.

- **Stakeholder feedback:** Collect direct feedback from stakeholders on the effectiveness of visual content in conveying ESG messages.

- **Reach analysis:** Evaluate the reach of visual content and its impact on raising awareness about the company's ESG initiatives.

With a well-developed visual communication and ESG strategy, the next step is to adapt and optimize these practices for the global context. In the next chapter, "**ADAPTING ESG COMMUNICATION TO THE GLOBAL CONTEXT**", we will explore how multinational companies can adapt their ESG communications to different cultures and local norms, ensuring messages are relevant and resonate with global audiences.

Remember: visual communication is not just a complement, but an integral part of the ESG communication strategy. As you move forward, use the power of images, videos, and design to bring your company's ESG initiatives to life, creating deeper, lasting connections with your stakeholders.

ADAPTING ESG COMMUNICATION TO THE GLOBAL CONTEXT

Multinational companies face the unique challenge of communicating their ESG initiatives in a way that is relevant and resonant across diverse cultural and geographic contexts. Adapting ESG messages to meet local expectations and norms is not just a matter of translation; it involves a deep understanding of the specific values, concerns and behaviors of each region. This chapter explores strategies for adapting ESG communication to the global context, ensuring that a company's sustainability practices are communicated effectively around the world.

UNDERSTANDING CULTURAL AND NORMATIVE DIFFERENCES

Before adapting ESG communications, it is crucial to understand the cultural and regulatory differences that can influence how messages are received in different regions:

- **Cultural research:** Conduct research to understand the specific attitudes, values and concerns related to ESG in different cultures.

- **Legal and regulatory standards:** Be aware of the different legal and regulatory standards regarding ESG that may exist in different countries.

ADAPTED COMMUNICATION STRATEGIES

Once cultural and regulatory nuances are understood, companies can employ several strategies to adapt their ESG communications:

- **Personalized messaging:** Develop messages that resonate with specific local concerns, using examples and case studies relevant to the region.

- **Local participation:** Involve local representatives in the communication process, ensuring that messages are presented in a way that is culturally appropriate and engaging.

- **Visual adaptation:** Adjust visual content, such as images and graphics, to reflect cultural diversity and ensure it is appropriate and relevant to local audiences.

CHALLENGES OF GLOBAL COMMUNICATION

When adapting ESG communication to the global context, companies can face several challenges, including:

- **Balance between coherence and personalization:** Maintain a globally coherent brand message, while adapting to local needs and expectations.

- **Risks of cultural misunderstandings:** Avoid misunderstandings or offenses that may arise from unrecognized cultural differences.

- **Communications logistics:** Manage the logistics of distributing tailored communications across multiple regions and languages.

MEASURING IMPACT AND ADJUSTING STRATEGIES

It is important to measure the impact of adapted ESG communications to ensure their effectiveness and make adjustments as necessary:

- **Local feedback:** Collect feedback from local stakeholders to assess the relevance and impact of communications.

- **Engagement analysis:** Monitor engagement with ESG content in different regions to identify what works well and what needs adjustment.

- **Ongoing reviews:** Conduct regular reviews of communication strategies to ensure they remain relevant and effective in different cultural and regulatory contexts.

With a carefully tailored approach to ESG communication in a global context, the next step is to address common challenges encountered when communicating ESG initiatives. In the next chapter, "**COMMON CHALLENGES IN ESG COMMUNICATION**", we will discuss how to identify, face and overcome obstacles often encountered when communicating sustainability and social responsibility practices.

Remember: Effective ESG communication on a global scale is not just about translating messages from one language to another, but about adapting those messages to resonate with cultural nuances and meet specific expectations. As you move forward, focus on creating communications that are truly global in their reach but locally relevant in their impact.

COMMON CHALLENGES IN ESG COMMUNICATION

Effectively communicating ESG initiatives can present a range of challenges, from overcoming the perception of "greenwashing" to engaging stakeholders with different levels of interest and understanding about ESG. This chapter addresses these common challenges and provides strategies for addressing and overcoming them, ensuring that communication of the company's sustainability and social responsibility practices is effective and impactful.

OVERCOMING THE PERCEPTION OF "GREENWASHING"

One of the biggest challenges in ESG communication is avoiding the perception of "greenwashing" — the practice of making unsubstantiated environmental claims to improve a company's public image. To overcome this challenge:

- **Base communications on evidence:** Ensure all ESG claims are supported by clear data and evidence.

- **Be transparent about challenges:** Communicate openly about challenges and limitations, in addition to successes, to build trust and credibility.

ENGAGING DIVERSE STAKEHOLDERS

Stakeholders range from employees and customers to investors and local communities, each with different expectations and levels of understanding about ESG. Strategies for effectively engaging include:

- **Personalized messages:** Adapt communication to meet the specific interests of different stakeholder groups.

- **Utilize multiple channels:** Employ a variety of communication channels to reach and engage stakeholders where they are most active.

NAVIGATING REGULATORY STANDARDS AND EXPECTATIONS

As the regulatory landscape for business sustainability continues to evolve, staying compliant and communicating effectively regarding regulations can be challenging. Useful strategies include:

- **Stay up to date:** Keep a close eye on changes to local and global ESG regulations.

- **Clear compliance communication:** Make sure you clearly communicate how your company is meeting or exceeding regulatory standards.

FIGHTING SUSTAINABILITY FATIGUE

With increased attention on sustainability, some audiences may experience "sustainability fatigue," becoming desensitized to messages about ESG. To combat this:

- **Innovate in messaging:** Find new and creative ways to communicate about ESG that capture attention and revitalize interest.

- **Emphasize actions and impact:** Focus on communicating concrete actions and their real impact, rather than just intentions or commitments.

BUILDING EFFECTIVE NARRATIVES

Constructing a compelling narrative that communicates a company's ESG journey can be difficult, but it is essential for effective communication. For that:

- **Tell real stories:** Use real case studies and success stories to illustrate the impact of ESG initiatives.

- **Show progress over time:** Document and share the ongoing progress of ESG initiatives, showing the company's evolution and long-term commitment.

Having covered strategies for overcoming common challenges in ESG communication, the next step is to look at real examples of success.

In the next chapter, **"FUTURE TRENDS IN ESG COMMUNICATION,"** we will explore the innovations and approaches that are shaping the future of communicating sustainability and social responsibility practices.

Remember: understanding and applying lessons from successful case studies can provide valuable direction and inspiration to enhance your own ESG communications strategies, enabling your company to not only tell its sustainability story effectively, but also inspire action and positive change.

FUTURE TRENDS IN ESG COMMUNICATION

As the world evolves, so does the field of ESG communications, with new trends emerging in response to changing stakeholder expectations, technological advances and global challenges. This chapter explores some of these future trends that are beginning to shape the future of communicating sustainability and social responsibility practices in companies.

AUGMENTED REALITY (AR) AND VIRTUAL REALITY (VR)

AR and VR offer immersive new ways to communicate ESG initiatives, allowing stakeholders to "experience" environmental and social impacts more directly. This could include virtual tours of renewable energy facilities or simulations that show the effects of global warming, providing a deeper, more emotional understanding of the challenges and solutions.

ARTIFICIAL INTELLIGENCE (AI) AND DATA ANALYSIS

AI and data analytics are becoming increasingly important tools in personalizing ESG communications, enabling companies to more effectively segment their audiences and deliver relevant content that addresses specific stakeholder concerns and interests. Additionally, AI can help monitor and analyze ESG performance in real time, offering insights that can be communicated in a transparent and up-to-date way.

PARTICIPATORY ENGAGEMENT PLATFORMS

Online platforms that promote participatory engagement, such as discussion forums and crowdfunding tools, are gaining popularity as ways to engage stakeholders in ESG initiatives. These platforms allow companies to collect ideas, feedback and even innovative solutions from a broad community, creating a sense of shared ownership and commitment to sustainability practices.

VALUES-BASED COMMUNICATION

As consumers become more aware and demanding of business

practices, values-based communication — which emphasizes alignment between company values and stakeholders' social and environmental concerns — will become even more critical. This involves communicating not just what the company is doing in terms of ESG, but why these actions reflect its core values.

TRANSPARENCY THROUGH BLOCKCHAIN

Blockchain technology offers new opportunities to increase transparency in ESG practices by providing an immutable and verifiable record of actions and results. This can include everything from supply chain traceability to carbon credit verification, offering stakeholders irrefutable proof of the company's commitment to sustainable and responsible practices.

With these future trends shaping the horizon for ESG communications, the next step is to reflect on how these innovations can be integrated into your company's communications strategies to create richer conversations, deeper engagement, and more meaningful action. In the next chapter, "**BUILDING A CAREER IN ESG CONSULTING**," we will turn our attention to professional development, exploring how individuals can build or advance their careers in the growing field of ESG consulting.

Remember: While the future of ESG communication is being shaped by technological advances and changing stakeholder expectations, the core of effective communication remains authenticity, transparency and a commitment to action. As you prepare for the future, keep looking for innovative ways to share your company's ESG journey, inspiring everyone involved to join you on this path toward sustainability.

BUILDING A CAREER IN ESG CONSULTING

As the importance of ESG practices continues to grow in the corporate world, there is a growing demand for qualified professionals capable of guiding companies on their sustainability and social responsibility journey. This chapter is dedicated to all those who want to build or advance their career in the field of ESG consultancy, providing insights into necessary skills, development opportunities and tips for professional success.

UNDERSTANDING THE FIELD OF ESG CONSULTING

ESG consulting involves advising companies on how to incorporate environmental, social and governance practices into their business operations and strategies. This may include:

- **ESG risk assessment:** Identify and evaluate risks related to environmental, social and governance factors that may affect the company.

- **Development of ESG strategies:** Assist in the development of strategies that align the company's operations and business objectives with sustainability principles.

- **Implementation and monitoring of ESG practices:** Help companies implement ESG practices and monitor their progress and effectiveness.

SKILLS REQUIRED FOR ESG CONSULTANTS

To become a successful ESG consultant, some key skills are required:

- **Technical knowledge in ESG:** An in-depth understanding of ESG topics and current trends in the field of sustainability.

- **Analytical skills:** Ability to analyze complex data and information to assess a company's ESG performance and identify areas for improvement.

- **Effective Communication:** Ability to communicate ESG

concepts clearly and persuasively, both in writing and verbally, to a variety of audiences.

- **Leadership and project management skills:** Ability to lead and manage ESG projects, coordinating multidisciplinary teams and ensuring the delivery of results within established deadlines.

- **Cultural sensitivity and adaptability:** For consultants working in a global context, understanding cultural differences and the ability to adapt ESG approaches to specific local contexts are crucial.

PROFESSIONAL DEVELOPMENT OPPORTUNITIES

The field of ESG consulting offers several professional development opportunities:

- **Continuing education:** Participate in courses, workshops and seminars specialized in ESG to improve knowledge and skills.

- **Professional certifications:** Obtaining recognized certifications in the ESG field can increase credibility and career opportunities.

- **Network:** Build a network of contacts in the ESG field by attending conferences, industry events and online discussion forums.

TIPS FOR SUCCESS IN AN ESG CONSULTING CAREER

- **Specialize:** Considering the breadth of the ESG field, specializing in a specific area (such as environmental sustainability, social responsibility or corporate governance) can differentiate you in the market.

- **Demonstrate impact:** Develop a portfolio that demonstrates your impact on previous ESG projects, including challenges overcome and results achieved.

- **Stay informed:** The field of ESG is constantly evolving. Staying up to date on the latest trends, regulations and best practices is essential.

- **Develop a strategic mindset:** In addition to technical knowledge, developing a strategic mindset that can connect ESG practices with a company's broader business objectives is crucial.

With the tools, knowledge and skills necessary to excel in ESG consultancy, the next step is to apply these insights into practice, contributing to the transformation of companies towards more sustainable and responsible operations. In the next chapter, **"THE JOURNEY TOWARDS EFFECTIVE ESG COMMUNICATION"**, we will reflect on the ongoing importance of developing and implementing ESG communication strategies for conscious companies.

Remember: starting a career in ESG consulting is not only a professional opportunity, but also a chance to significantly contribute to a more sustainable and fair future. As you move forward, commit to learning, growing, and making a difference in the world, one ESG project at a time.

THE JOURNEY TOWARDS EFFECTIVE ESG COMMUNICATION

Throughout this guide, we explore the complexity and importance of developing and implementing effective communication strategies for companies committed to ESG practices. From understanding the fundamentals of ESG to adapting strategies for a global context, we emphasize the need for authenticity, transparency and engagement in communicating sustainability and social responsibility initiatives.

REFLECTING ON THE JOURNEY

This journey has led us to recognize that ESG communication is not just a matter of reporting actions or complying with regulations; it's about telling a story that resonates with stakeholders, inspiring trust, action and change. The previous chapters have provided a solid foundation for understanding how each aspect of ESG practices can be communicated effectively, from selecting communication channels to addressing common challenges.

LOOKING TO THE FUTURE

As we move forward, it is clear that ESG communication will continue to evolve. Emerging trends, such as the use of advanced technologies and the growing demand for transparency, will shape future strategies. To stay ahead, companies will need to be agile, adaptable and committed to continually improving their sustainability practices.

MAKING THE DIFFERENCE

Each of us has a role to play in promoting a more sustainable future. Whether as consultants, communicators or conscious citizens, our approach to ESG communication can significantly influence the way sustainability practices are perceived and implemented. Committing to ongoing education, the pursuit of innovation, and collaboration across industries and cultures are essential steps to making a difference.

This guide is an invitation to explore, learn and grow in the area of ESG communications. We thank everyone who embarked on this journey with us, seeking not only to improve their professional skills, but also to contribute to positive change in the world. Together, we can tackle the sustainability challenges of our time and inspire others to join us in this crucial cause.

Remember, the journey to effective ESG communication is ongoing and full of opportunities for innovation and impact. We encourage you to continue seeking knowledge, sharing your experiences and working to integrate ESG practices into the heart of business and communications strategies. In doing so, we will not only strengthen the brands and companies we work for, but we will also contribute to a fairer, more sustainable and prosperous world for all.

With this concluding chapter, we hope we have provided you with the tools and inspiration you need to move forward on your ESG communications journey, armed with the knowledge, skills and passion to make a difference. The future of sustainability in companies is in our hands, and together, we can create a narrative of positive and lasting change.

As we turn the final page of this journey together, I sincerely hope that the learnings shared here have touched your heart and sparked new perspectives. If this book has brought you any value, I kindly ask that you take a few moments to leave a review on Amazon. Your words not only help me grow and hone my craft, but they also guide other readers in their quests for knowledge and inspiration. Your opinion is a valuable gift, both for me and for the community of readers looking for stories that transform. I sincerely thank you for sharing this journey with me and I hope we can meet again in the pages of a new adventure.

REGINALDO OSNILDO

Hello, I'm Reginaldo Osnildo, author and innovator in the fields of sales, technology, and communication strategies. My background spans from the academic setting, as a professor and researcher at the University of Southern Santa Catarina, to hands-on strategy development at the Catarinense Radio Group. With a PhD in sales narratives and digital convergence, and a Master's in storytelling and social imaginary, I offer my readers a unique blend of theory and practice. My aim is to deliver knowledge in a simple, practical, and didactic language, encouraging direct application in one's personal and professional life.

Yours sincerely

Reginaldo Osnildo

+55 48 991913865

reginaldoosnildo@gmail.com

www.ingramcontent.com/pod-product-compliance
Lightning Source LLC
Chambersburg PA
CBHW050326230526
45471CB00005B/2377